Published in the United States of America by The Child's World®
PO Box 326 • Chanhassen, MN 55317-0326
800-599-READ • www.childsworld.com

My First Steps to Math™ is a registered trademark of Scholastic, Inc.

Library of Congress Cataloging-in-Publication Data
Moncure, Jane Belk.
My one book / by Jane Belk Moncure.
p. cm. — (My first steps to math)
ISBN 1-59296-656-X (lib. bdg. : alk. paper)
1. Counting—Juvenile literature. 2. Number concept—Juvenile literature. I. Title.
QA113.M666 2006
513.2'11—dc22
2005025691

My  Book

by Jane Belk Moncure

illustrated by Ben Mahan

This is Little one .

Little  lives in . . .

the house of one.

The house of one has one room.

He sits at one table.
He drinks one glass
of milk. He eats one
bowl of soup . . .

one slice of cake, and one apple.

Each day Little  goes for a walk.

He hops one hop. Can you?

He jumps one jump. Can you?

He smells one little flower. Can you?

One day he finds . . .

one tree,

one acorn,

and one squirrel.

He gives the acorn to the squirrel.

Then Little one finds

one unicorn.

He claps one clap. Can you?

Little  finds one wagon.

"The unicorn can pull my wagon," he says.

Little finds . . .

one mouse.

"Come, ride in my wagon," he says.
The mouse squeaks one squeak. Can you?

Next he finds . . .

one kitten.

The kitten is sad.
"Come, ride in my wagon," says Little one.

One mouse jumps out.

How many kittens jump in?

Now Little one finds . . .

one puppy.

The puppy is sad.

"Come, ride in my wagon,"

says Little  .

How many kittens jump out?

How many puppies jump in?

One happy puppy barks one little bark.
Can you?

Then Little  sees . . .

one  star in the sky.

"We must go home,"
he says.

Away they go.

Little  gives the unicorn one pat on the head . . .

and one bucket of corn.

He gives the puppy

one bone . . .

and one hug.

He eats one peanut butter and jelly sandwich . . .

and drinks one cup of hot cocoa.

Little  jumps into one little bed . . .

with one big jump. Can you?

He pulls up
one blanket,

winks one wink,

turns off one light,

and says, "Good night." Can you?

Little  finds one of everything.

one flower

one tree

one acorn

one squirrel

one star

one wagon

one mouse

one kitten

one puppy

Now you find one thing.

Let's add with Little  one.

 +  =

I + 0 = I

Now take away.

 −  =

I − I = 0

Little  makes a I this way.

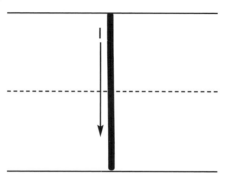

Then he makes the number word like this:

You can make them in the air with your finger.